READING
and
WRITING
in the
REAL WORLD

A Handbook of High Interest
and Fun Activities for Your Students

by Irene H. Blum,
Nancy E. Taylor and Priscilla P. Waynant

Editor: Maureen H. Cook
Layout: M. Jane Smyth
Illustrations: Joy Friedman
Cover: Jim Stewart

Library of Congress Cataloging in Publication Data

Blum, Irene H.
  Reading and writing in the real world.

  Bibliography: p 94-95
  1. Reading games.   I. Taylor, Nancy E.
II. Waynant, Priscilla P.   III. Title.
LB1050.4.B64   372.4'1   81-8252
ISBN 0-07-530315-9   AACR2

Published by Instructo/McGraw-Hill, Paoli, Pennsylvania 19301

10 9 8 7 6 5 4 3 2 1

Acknowledgements

For some time we have wanted to write a "practical" book that would reflect our philosophy of literacy acquisition. We wanted a book that would provide practical ideas as well as a strong rationale for the activities suggested. Since our philosophy reflects a global, wholistic view of learning there is no hierarchically ordered sequence of learning experiences. Rather, four basic concepts or understandings provide the framework for the suggestions.

Many people contributed to the ideas expressed in this book. We especially want to note the contribution and inspiration of Gail Moeller. Her work exhibits one of the finest understandings we have ever encountered of how to make written language relevant and alive to children. In addition we would like to thank all the teachers who worked with us during the 1979-1980 school year to incorporate the framework into a correct curriculum. Particular thanks go to Anne Derricotte, Joan Coble, Johnsie Evans, Anne Gay and Mary Jo Nash.

Irene Blum
Nancy E. Taylor
Priscilla P. Waynant

Contents

INTRODUCTION

Ideas to Help Children Develop Reading and Writing Skills

The world is full of opportunities to read and write. This book is designed for teachers and parents who want to capitalize on these real-world opportunities and, in the process, foster the development of children's reading and writing skills in a meaningful way.

Two fundamental notions underly the activities in this book.

- **Children need to see a connection between their world and activities that involve reading and writing.** Activities that relate reading and writing to the child's world help children learn the purposes that reading and writing serve.
- **Children's definitions of reading and writing should be broad.** Unfortunately, many children view reading as something they do in school when they read aloud in a group. Such views tend to lead to overconcern with precision and skill at the expense of meaning.

In a similar manner many children develop a distaste for writing because of school and home emphasis on correctness. Few adults would like to have their first drafts of business letters or shopping lists subjected to the standards we frequently impose on children's writing.

This book provides concrete examples of activities that will help children develop broad conceptions of reading and writing and see these skills as functionally relevant in their lives. The descriptions of activities are presented in a way that makes clear both the rationale for the activity and the characteristics of the instructional environment that will best convey the functional nature of the activity.

Both parents and teachers are concerned with helping children to read for meaning and to develop a desire to communicate through print. This book is based on the position that reading and writing activities which stress the importance of print as a means of communicating a message or idea will help children develop a desire to orientation to print. There is considerable theoretical and research support for this position. Some pertinent articles that elaborate this argument are listed in the suggested readings at the end of this section. The activities in this book are organized around three ideas on reading and writing that we feel good readers and writers understand:

- written language conveys a message
- the purposes for reading and writing are many and varied
- written language needs to be more explicit than spoken language

Children develop these understandings from wide and appropriate experiences with print. The encounters with print generate a type of learning that cannot be taught by telling. The activities that follow serve as examples to parents and teachers. Others will come to mind as you try this type of teaching...the world is full of opportunities to read and write.

How To Use This Book

This small book serves a two-fold purpose:
1. To identify some basic understandings children need to develop if they are to become efficient readers and writers.
2. To provide teachers with motivating and effective activities they can use in their classrooms to foster those understandings.

We feel that it is paramount that the users of this book not lose sight of the fact that the activities are only means to an end: the development of these basic understandings about reading and writing. If teachers keep this goal in mind as they select and use the activities, students will develop these important understandings, and teachers will find that other ideas and activities will readily suggest themselves.

The format of the book provides a short rationale for each understanding, followed by activities that can be used in the classroom. Each teacher activity is followed in turn by a **Parent Miniplan** that can be sent home with students. These plans are designed to extend school learnings into the home. Many of the ideas in the parent miniplans are suitable for the classroom and might also be used there. We feel strongly, however, that the use of the parent miniplans has major benefits for teachers and students. First, the use of these plans will help students see the relevance of reading and writing in their lives beyond the classroom. Second, the miniplans help parents reinforce basic skill development in meaningful and appropriate ways. Third, these plans represent a concrete and easily implemented cooperative link between home and school.

Teachers will probably want to explain the intent of the Parent Miniplans and their relationship to classroom activities. This could be done at beginning of the year conferences, grade level meetings, or by sending an introductory message (such as the sample which follows).

Dear Parents,

During this school year, we will be working on many different activities which stress the idea that print is used to communicate a message or ideas so that children will appreciate the usefulness of reading and writing. Two fundamental notions underlie these activities:

1. **Children need to see a connection between their world and activities that involve reading and writing.** Activities that relate reading and writing to the child's world help children learn the purposes that reading and writing serve.

2. **Children's definition of reading and writing should be broad.** Unfortunately, many children view reading as something they do in school when they read aloud in a group. Such views sometimes lead to overconcern with precision and skill at the expense of meaning.

All kinds of learning require practice. "The more you practice, the better you get" is a familiar saying to all of us. From time to time, I will be sending home **Parent Miniplans** that serve as followup (practice) for school activities. Each Parent Miniplan has a short rationale which explains the purpose and directions for completing each activity. These home activities use easily available materials and suggest ways of using everyday situations as learning experiences. Your child will be practicing reading and writing in natural, meaningful and comfortable situations. Be sure to tell your child the things she or he is doing well so that she or he will feel successful. You will both enjoy the activities even more as you see the child making progress.

Thank you for your cooperation.

CHAPTER 1
Written Language Conveys a Message

Stop and think about it ... all writing serves to convey a message. Whether a label or letter, the writer encoded a message to be transmitted to another person. This basic notion underlying written communication is sometimes not apparent to young readers.

There are a number of reasons why young children may not recognize this basic characteristic of writing.

First, written language serves purposes for those who are already literate. Some degree of skill with written language is required before the use of written language takes priority over spoken language in situations where written language is naturally more efficient and appropriate. In a similar fashion, individuals who are skilled at typing will use the machine for composing almost all of their written communication, while those less skilled will rarely use the typewriter unless a typed product is required.

Second, because written language serves the purpose of those who are literate and because literacy is generally associated with adulthood, children's experiences with the written word are usually closely associated with and dependent upon experiences with adults. There is also evidence that attention to print may depend largely on the spontaneous teaching behavior of parents and other adults (Hiebert, 1980).

Children may be immersed in a world of print, but they may not discover the usefulness of print without an adult's help. In helping children understand the communicative functions of print, adults must focus on print in situations that are relevant to the child. Many conventional instructional reading activities fail to do this because they reflect adult rather than child foci. All of us have seen primary classrooms that label doors, windows, pencil sharpeners, desks, and other classroom objects in hope that the young readers will incorporate these words into their sight vocabulary. Frequently, however, these efforts result in little gain because they neglect a critical aspect: the labels serve no function in the child's life. Children do not need to use the print to identify the referent. Adults, on the other hand, rely on labels to help them quickly identify a needed object among many objects (a particular spice on a spice rack or a particular shoe size among many boxes of the same style), to help them sort objects in particular places (filing systems, library systems, and so on), or to help them remember names, things, dates and places, such as phone books, grocery lists and calenders.

If children are to recognize the message-conveying aspect of written language, they must encounter written language in situations where the text performs a functional purpose.

All of the activities in this book stress the underlying notion of communicative intention. Those that are grouped together in this section are those that make this idea particularly apparent.

MESSAGE CENTER

WHY: Sending and receiving messages (or mail) is perhaps the most direct and obvious way of becoming aware of the function of written language in communicating with someone not immediately present. Both personal and business messages are appropriate content.

Using a classroom message center provides an opportunity for children to practice reading and writing skills in a functional situation.

WITH: Bulletin board, note paper, pencils, thumbtacks.

HOW: 1. Begin sending individual messages to children in your class as early in the school year as possible. If you have access to a class list prior to the opening of school, children would probably be delighted to receive a "hello" note from their new teacher. You might include a name tag for the first few days of school. If it is not possible to mail notes ahead, you can have welcoming messages with name tags enclosed posted at your classroom message center. As children arrive on the first day, help them locate their message.

2. After the first day, you will probably want to limit the number of messages posted each day, but use the message center as another way of communicating and helping children recognize that notes are an alternative to talking. You might send directions for an individual or small group activity (e.g., *Dear Alan, please be sure to go over your math practice sheets before our conference this afternoon.*).

3. You will probably be the major message writer at the beginning of the year, but as time goes by, encourage children to respond to your messages and to send messages to one another.

WHAT ELSE: Use the message center for public communication from time to time. You could note when a group does an especially good job or let the class know about some special event that is coming up.

Notes to a Friend

WHY: Receiving and sending messages is probably the most direct way of helping children recognize that writing is another way of communicating when talking is not possible.

HOW: 1. Arrange with an out-of-town relative or friend to exchange a series of notes with your child.

2. Talk with your child about the news and information that can be included to let the correspondent know about important things in the child's life. The child can either write or dictate the message.

3. Provide whatever help is needed in reading and responding to notes that are received.

WHAT ELSE: 1. Your child can collect the notes and display them in a scrapbook or collage.

2. As your child becomes more involved in the note writing, you can point out the proper form for letter headings and addresses.

3. Encourage the child to become a pen pal.

4. Leave special messages around the house for your child: *Diane, be sure to put your napkin in the napkin ring when you finish.*

BALLOON A MESSAGE

WHY: Communicating to people not present is one major function of written language. Sending off messages in helium-filled balloons provides a motivating situation to make children understand this function. Since it involves two-way communication, the activity is doubly effective.

WITH: Balloon, helium tank, sturdy string, postcard, stamp.

HOW: 1. Start with a discussion of the purpose of the activity: to send up balloons and trace their path and distance. Students should discuss the type of information to provide and the type of information they want to get back.

2. Students design a postcard that tells the receiver who they are and what to do with the postcard when he or she finds the balloon.

Example:

Sender:

My name is _____

I live at _____

I sent this postcard in a helium-filled balloon

on _____ at _____ from _____.

Would you please fill out the information and mail the postcard back to me.

Receiver:

My name is _____

I live at _____

I found your balloon on _____ at _____ in _____.

3. Self-address and stamp the postcard.

4. Securely attach the postcard to a helium-filled balloon. (You may want to enclose the postcard in a zip-lock plastic bag for protection.)

5. Go to your designated "launch site" and send off the balloon.

WHAT ELSE:

1. Children can locate the "touch down" spot of returned postcards on a map, then learn how to use the map to figure out how far their postcards travelled.

2. Children can write a thank-you note to the person who found the balloon.

3. If **Balloon a Message** is done as a classroom activity, children can use maps to find out whose message travelled the farthest distance.

4. Results of map activites can be plotted on graphs and charts related to distance and time. For example, one chart might plot each child's name and the "launch site" against the "landing site". Another might plot time factors, e.g., whose card was returned first.

Pop a Message

WHY: Notes and messages of various kinds help to highlight the communication value of written language. A related activity that you might want to try at home can be used as a family project or as a party game.

HOW: 1. Write out simple but specific directions for situations that children can act out (e.g., act like a duck, jump three times; climb a beanstalk) on sheets of note or memo paper.

2. Fold the slips of paper and insert them in deflated balloons. Blow up the balloons and knot the ends. Attach the balloons to a long string or put them in a basket.

3. Have each participant choose a balloon. One at a time, each person punctures a balloon, then acts out the instructions inside. Other family members or party guests try to guess what is being dramatized. Be sure someone is available to assist with reading and planning the dramatization.

TALKING TEE SHIRT

WHY: Tee shirts have become anyone's commercial. Shirts are carefully looked over to find the one that conveys just the right message to all who encounter the wearer. Designing their own tee shirt message is an excellent way to get the communication intent of written language across to students.

WITH: Tee shirts, permanent felt-tip markers.

HOW: 1. Have children bring in tee shirts which have a motto or message. Discuss the nature of the messages and the way in which people have played around with language to make a point or communicate a message for public knowledge.

2. Brainstorm or have children work in small groups to generate mottos or slogans they would like to print on a tee shirt (e.g., for first graders, "We're #1; for second graders, "We're second to none."; for third graders, "We deserve three cheers.").

3. Children can vote to select a class slogan from the set the class generated, then copy the slogan onto a tee shirt using the felt-tip marker.

WHAT ELSE: 1. Tie-dying or silk screening are a little more complicated but would be super.

2. Developing a poster or bumper sticker for the class is a similar activity children might enjoy.

3. You can extend this activity with a school-wide project or contest to publicize a school event or develop a school slogan.

4. Have a "Wear-Our-Tee-Shirts-Day" for all to sport their tee shirts.

The Writing Wall

WHY: Over-reliance on modern technology makes it less common to use writing as a means of self-expression. We are much more likely to use the telephone than write a letter to express either pleasure or dissatisfaction with a product or service. Yet writing remains a very powerful vehicle for expressing feelings and opinions. It is only with opportunity and encouragement for practice that children will come to recognize and participate in this aspect of writing.

HOW: 1. Use masking tape to tape up a "wall-long" sheet of brown wrapping paper on a large empty wall in your home. Stock a container such as a basket or an empty coffee can with colored pencils, marking pens, chalk and crayons (the more variety the better). Add unusual writing implements as they can frequently motivate a child to write.

2. You will probably want to make the ground rules clear for this activity: write only on the writing wall, and be sure the writing is suitable for "public consumption".

3. Encourage your child to express him- or herself in writing. He or she can record important events: *Don't forget soccer practice on Tuesday*; or note reactions to daily experience: *Dinner was really great today*; or make public invitations. Parents play a big role in getting the wall started and keeping up the interest. Messages like *Does anyone want to go to the movies this weekend?* are sure to get a response.

4. Change the paper when it is full.

WHAT ELSE: 1. Save the sheets of paper and, as time goes by, review them with your child. Compare the writing and note if the child is using different patterns and longer phrases.

2. Paint one wall of a playroom or child's bedroom with two coats of chalkboard paint to make the child a personal giant-sized chalkboard.

READ IT AGAIN, SAM

WHY: Just as in learning anything else, the more children practice reading, the better they will be able to read. Children seem to spontaneously seek the practice they need when trying to master a new task, such as completing a puzzle. When children work on new puzzles, they usually look at the picture of the completed puzzle, dump the pieces, then work to reassemble the pattern or pictures. When they complete the task, they very often dump the pieces immediately and begin again, each time completing the puzzle more quickly and easily.

Rereading is an analogous strategy for the beginning and/or problem reader. The teacher provides a model of fluent reading of a passage so that the reader knows what to work toward. Children are encouraged to read aloud several times, with help if they ask for it, so that their reading will become more fluent.

WITH: A high-interest passage at the child's instructional level. The passage can be from basal materials you are using in class or from material selected by the child. For this activity, one or two connected sentences are sufficient, but the passage should be no longer than 75 words. Going back to the puzzle analogy, if the puzzle is far too complex, the youngster is likely to give up.

HOW: 1. Identify a passage.

2. Explain that the child will reread the passage several times so that the reading will get better and better.

3. Read the passage aloud while the child follows along.

4. Read the passage again, this time having the child read along.

5. Have the child read the passage at least twice. If the child wants to and time permits, she or he can do additional rereadings.
   - If the child wants help with a word, she or he can ask.
   - If the child makes more than five mistakes, this passage is too difficult and another passage should be selected.

6. Each time the child reads, comment on how the reading is changing and improving.

WHAT ELSE: 1. You might want to provide an evaluation sheet so that the child can rate each reading and then note the change.

2. If you want to use rereading with your instructional materials, you could read the instructional passage aloud to a reading group, then have the children practice rereading in pairs.

3. Tape a favorite story and put this tape and book at a listening center so that children can read along while they listen for a similar practice experience. Many read-along materials are available commercially (see Bibliography).

4. After practicing a passage, children might enjoy taping their reading or presenting the passage to another child or small group.

5. Some children might enjoy using the tape recorder to compare first and later readings of a passage.

Just One More Time

WHY: Just as in learning anything else, the more children practice reading, the better they will be able to read. Children seem to spontaneously seek the practice they need when trying to master a new task, such as riding a bike. They are willing to try again and again with a little help and a clear goal in mind.

Rereading provides practice to help a child become a fluent reader. Be sure to tell your child the things she or he is doing well so that the child will feel successful as a reader.

HOW: 1. Use a high-interest passage that the teacher recommends or that the child selects. (For this activity, one or two connected sentences are sufficient, but the passage should be no longer than 75 words.)

2. Explain to the child that she or he will be reading the passage several times so that the reading will get better and better.

3. Read the passage aloud while the child follows along.

4. Read the passage again, this time having the child read along.

5. Have the child read the passage at least twice. If the child wants to, she or he can do additional readings.

   • If the child needs help with a word, give it.
   • If the child makes more than five mistakes, this passage is too difficult and another passage should be selected.

6. Each time the child reads, comment on how the reading is changing and improving.

WHAT ELSE: Different family members could each prepare a passage from a story or poem and do the reading as a family project.

STORY TIME

WHY: The very best way to help young children learn to read is to give them as much experience with meaningful print as possible. Reading to them is one of the most enjoyable ways to develop the desire to learn in children.

WITH: A variety of books.

HOW: Select a time each day to read a book that you (or the children) have selected. In order for daily story reading to be a success, you must give careful consideration to the time you select, the attention span and interests of the audience, and the choice of story. Remember, this is a very important learning activity; select a time when children will be relaxed and able to focus their attention. Have them come to a special place in the room or area of the rug. Present stories you like and prepare by prereading so that the presentation is lively and animated.

WHAT ELSE: 1. Discussion following the story is often a time for extending concepts and sharing ideas. You can take advantage of this opportunity by selecting a series of books which focus on a concept or theme or several books by the same author.

2. Children often enjoy hearing stories repeated several times. These stories can be extended with a variety of creative dramatic activities: spontaneous dramatization, puppet shows and pantomime.

3. In addition to hearing stories, children enjoy looking at books, retelling and/or reading them. Many teachers plan a daily independent reading time (or for young children, time with books) in addition to story reading. Books you may have read at story time can be made available along with other materials from your classroom library for this activity.

4. Tape a particular favorite and put the book and tape at the listening center so that children can listen and read.

5. Let the children select a day when they will share a favorite book. With young children, their presentation might simply be the title, author, and showing a favorite picture or reading one or two favorite pages, rather than trying to read an entire story.

6. Invite parents to read to small groups of children during story time.

Reading Time

WHY: One of the simplest, but perhaps the most important things you can do to encourage your child's success in learning to read is to READ TO YOUR CHILD! Five or ten minutes spent reading books that you and your child select will yield enormous benefits. Show your child that you enjoy reading and make reading time a part of each day.

HOW: 1. Set aside a special time each day to read to your child. For families with more than one child, reading time can be a nice way to spend a special few minutes with each child individually. This activity enables children to enjoy participating in a reading activity. It is also an important learning activity.

2. Plan the time and place so that you are both relaxed and can focus attention.

3. Try to sit so that the child can see the text and pictures while you are reading.

4. Choose stories and books that you will enjoy reading aloud. You may want to start with some that were your favorites as a child. Let the child share in selecting materials, too. She or he may suggest stories read in school or the original story on which a movie or television show is based. Your child's teacher and librarians are willing and able resources.

WHAT ELSE: 1. Children often enjoy hearing the same story over and over. As children become more familiar with the text, let them say the character's names, highly predictable words that complete a sentence, or phrases that are repeated in certain stories.

2. Let the child retell the story, using pictures and as much of the text as she or he can for clues.

3. Explain unfamiliar or unusual vocabulary and compare stories with one another. This kind of discussion extends concepts and ideas.

4. Even after children have learned to read, they will enjoy being read to. You could choose books they cannot read independently but can understand.

BE THE STORYTELLER

WHY: Children enjoy listening to and reading good literature. These favorite stories can be used to provide important learning experiences. Having children retell a story (in their own words) provides a way for them to demonstrate their understanding and interpretation.

WITH: Favorite children's books.

HOW: 1. Select a story for the retelling activity. You may choose to use a story you read to the whole class, but for the retelling activity, work with a small group.

2. Discuss the story with the group. The important features of your discussion will, of course, depend on the story. For example, if you are discussing Beatrix Potter's *Peter Rabbit*, you might focus on characters and development of the story. With many stories, such as *The Three Bears*, sequence is a very important feature.

3. Have children write or dictate as much of the story as they can in their own words.

- Some children find it very useful to make an illustration or series of illustrations prior to writing. This serves as a type of "rehearsal" for the retelling or writing.
- A series of key words or phrases may serve as the initial draft for less skilled writers. This is an important first step. Help children recognize that one of the major advantages of writing is that you can revise and alter before producing a finished draft.

4. Reread each child's work, encouraging revision and elaboration.

5. Have the child read the retelling to you and/or to another child in the group.

WHAT ELSE: 1. Type or have the children recopy a finished draft of their retelling. Assemble several children's work for a bulletin board display or group book.

2. Children might enjoy "presenting" their version of a story to another reading group or to the class.

3. Have children read and compare one another's retellings of favorite stories.

4. Prior to retelling, have the children dramatize the story. Acting out requires attention to detail, and the retelling may be quite a bit more elaborate.

And That's the Way It Is

WHY: The books you've read to children can be the basis for important discoveries beyond the pure pleasure of a good story. Having children retell a story in their own words provides a way for them to demonstrate their understanding and interpretation.

HOW: 1. With your child, choose a selection the child has heard several times. The first time you try this, choose an old favorite with familiar characters.

2. Have the child pretend she or he is the main character, telling the story to a newspaper reporter. The parent, taking the role of the reporter records the story.

- Having the child write or dictate in her or his own words generates content for beginning reading passages which is certain to contain familiar vocabulary and language patterns. Record the child's language exactly as dictated—this is an interview—and be sure to reread the child's version with him or her several times.
- You will probably want to start with one incident or episode rather than an entire story for retelling.

WHAT ELSE: 1. If you have a tape recorder available, tape the child's story. She or he will enjoy listening to it, and transcribing may be simpler from a tape than trying to write as the child talks.

2. The child might enjoy recopying his or her own version of the story. Just before recopying, encourage the child to think about making any corrections or changes.

WHAT'S IN A WORD

WHY: Very often, good literature provides a model of written language which employs richer and more varied vocabulary than is typically used in oral language. **What's In a Word** is an activity aimed at capitalizing on and extending exposure to this expanded vocabulary.

WITH: William Steig's *Sylvester and the Magic Pebble* or *The Amazing Bone* or other similar stories (see Bibliography).

HOW: 1. After reading a selection, have the children brainstorm a list of words they found unusual or interesting or unfamiliar. You may need to help by rereading or highlighting words in context as you present the material.

2. As children generate the word list, write each suggested word on the chalkboard or on chart paper.

3. Reread the words, pointing to or framing each one as you read it.

4. Have children come to the board or chart and point out words they can read or ask for volunteers to come and point out words you name.

5. Following this group work, each child selects one word to illustrate with a picture or design.

6. As children complete the illustrations or designs, they write or dictate a caption. The caption can be one word, or phrase, or a more complex piece of writing. Encourage children to be as independent as possible as soon as possible. For example, even beginning writers can use the word list as a spelling resource.

WHAT ELSE: 1. Use the captioned artwork for a bulletin board display.

2. Assemble a set of captioned pictures into a group book with a list of the new words on the inside of the front cover.
- Be sure to use the book during instructional reading time to make it assigned reading.
- Put the group book into the classroom library, available to be checked out.
- When a child demonstrates that she or he can read the entire book, have her or him take it home overnight to read to parents.

3. Use the captioned pictures as the basis for a more elaborate story.

Refrigerator Dictionary

WHY: The vocabulary in good literature is often more colorful and unusual than the vocabulary typically used in conversation. Reading to children will expose them to a rich and varied model of written language. **Refrigerator Dictionary** is an activity to encourage children to incorporate some of the new terms encountered into their speaking and writing vocabulary.

HOW: 1. When you read a book with unusual or particularly colorful vocabulary, choose one or two words to be your "refrigerator vocabulary" for the week.

2. Have the child write the word you select at the top of a large sheet of paper.

3. Post the word on the refrigerator using a magnetic clip or tape.

4. Try to use the word in a new sentence at least once each day. Have the child write or dictate each day's sentence under the word.

WHAT ELSE: 1. Keep a record of the number of times a child uses the word correctly.

2. If your family enjoys competition, offer a small reward or treat to the person who uses the new word correctly most often.

3. You can add variety to your vocabulary stretching by having the family try to avoid some overused terms. For example, post the word "good" on the refrigerator and make that word "Taboo" for the day. Generate some alternative terms, such as *fine, swell, wonderful,* and list these on the same paper or chart. Keep a list of the words used in place of the taboo word.

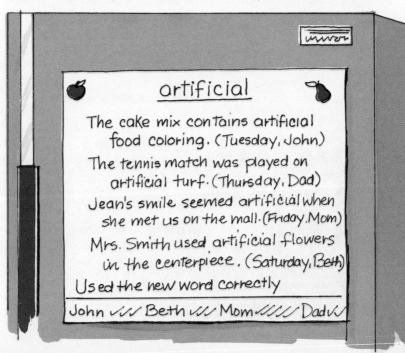

MODELING ON LITERATURE

WHY: Along with rich and varied vocabulary, good literature also provides a model of more complex language patterns. Children who are familiar with effective and expressive writing can be encouraged to incorporate important elements into their own works.

WITH: Books, such as Barbara Emberly's *Drummer Hoff* or Rosemary Wells' *Noisy Nora,* repeat a language pattern (see Bibliography). Following several readings of such a book, help children identify and locate the pattern that is required. For example, there is a rhythm and rhyme pattern in the book *Drummer Hoff.*

Drummer Hoff fired it off.

Private Parriage
brought the carriage
but Drummer Hoff fired it off.

HOW: 1. Have children work in pairs to generate another example of the pattern (e.g., *Mr. Brown is a clown.*). Then, have each pair write or dictate its work.

2. After sharing each pair's work, combine them into a group book.

WHAT ELSE: Put the group books developed by your class with the book that served as a model in the reading area. Encourage children to read and compare the two versions.

Real World ABC and 1, 2, 3,

WHY: Children who have opportunities to listen to and/or read examples of effective written language will have concrete examples to model in their own writing.

HOW: 1. Read an alphabet book or a counting book to your child.

2. With the child, develop a personal "real-world" alphabet or counting book using pictures of familiar items from labels or magazine ads. An alphabet book might include: *A (Apple Juice); B (Baked Beans); C (Chicken Soup).* A counting book might illustrate: *1(tricycle); 2 (balls); 3 (coats);* with pictures and print from a magazine or catalog collection.

3. Be sure the pictures include labeling print or label them yourself.

WHAT ELSE: 1. Several commonly available books focus on the real world and might be used as examples: Patricia Ruben's *Apples to Zippers* and Tana Hoban's *Count and See* (see Bibliography).

2. Another type of book you might want to model repeats a particular phrase or language pattern. Children can develop a "real-world" version that imitates a similar pattern (e.g. Eric Carle's *The Very Hungry Caterpillar* could be imitated with a "real-world" version called "Going Grocery Shopping With Dad" in which children select one item to shop for on Monday, two items on Tuesday, and so on).

FOUND FOUND FOUND

WHY: Children use oral language in situations where the listener is already familiar with the context. In learning to use written language children must learn to employ language that is much more elaborate and descriptive. Lost and found articles, a common experience in the school setting, provide a wonderful opportunity for children to develop an awareness for the need for clear description.

Describing articles that have been found is the most concrete way to start. The members of the class have the actual article before them and can compare their descriptions to the article.

WITH: Newspapers, Found Form (below).

HOW: 1. Bring in classified ads from a newspaper to have the children read and notice how the ads are written.

2. Have enough copies of the Found Form for each child to use for an article of clothing or item found at school.

FOUND FOUND FOUND

Item Description: _____

_____

Found Where _____

Found When _____

Contact _____

Telephone # _____ Grade ____

Room ____

---

3. Reserve a section of the Hall Bulletin Board for posting the *Found* notices.

4. As the items are returned to the rightful owner, have the children remove the notice from the board.

PLEASE TAKE ALL PURCHASES TO CHECK-OUT TABLE

250 PIECES PUZZLE

BINGO

Garage Sale

WHY: Written information can communicate to a larger audience faster than verbal communication. Advertising is a very familiar example of this. The need for detail and clear description in writing is very obvious in the advertising example. Participation in preparing a catalog of items and posters or signs for a family garage sale provides an opportunity to practice and develop skill in this type of writing.

HOW: 1. As a family, search through the house for obsolete items that can be used in a garage sale.

2. In order to advertise the items for sale, develop a catalog listing the items with a description of each and an approximate cost.

Example: *Tricycle*, small, 18", red tricycle in good condition with a fine silver bell. $4.50

Have the catalog available at the sale location so that customers can preview all the items or look for particular items they want.

3. Prepare multiple copies of a flyer advertising the date, place, and time of the sale.

4. Using large tagboard, make up attractive signs that advertise the garage sale. Post signs at various *busy* intersections and closer to the sale's location. Be sure the signs list the date of the sale, the time and the location of the sale.

GARAGE
SALE

9:00 am to 6:00 pm

Nov. 1st

6565 Pennapaste Court
Coppersville, MD 21111

5. Set up tables to display the items and make place cards noting the price asked for each item.

6. Plan to have a check-out station where the cashier will collect the money for the purchased items. Make a sign to denote the check-out station. If you will accept a check for payment, note on the sign how to make out the check.

CHECK-OUT
STATION

Cash or Check

Make checks payable to:

_____

Be sure your name, address and telephone number appear on the check.

7. Proceeds from the garage sale can be divided among family members who worked on the sale.

WHAT ELSE: 1. Duplicating and distributing your catalog and flyers will enable you to reach a larger audience. Reasonably priced duplicating facilities are available in many libraries and post offices.

2. Items not sold at the garage sale can be relisted with the description and an "adjusted" price in order to have a "Final Sale with Prices Drastically Reduced". This new flyer can be passed out from house to house. Announced on this flyer a final sale date or, if you prefer, a phone number to call between designated hours for inquiring about the items for sale.

LOST LOST LOST

WHY: Describing an article that has been lost is more difficult since the student doesn't have the actual object to guide the description. Once students can generate descriptions for found items, writing ads for lost items would be a challenging next step.

WITH: Newspaper ads, lost items from classmates, school bulletin board, PA System.

HOW: Have the children pair up (or group) to write a classified ad for a school bulletin regarding a lost item.

1. Bring in newspaper ads for children to read to get a notion of how to write a clear, concise ad.

2. After children identify lost items, have them work in groups to brainstorm important features that will help identify their lost possessions.

3. Have each child write a two or three line ad, using the newspaper ads as a model.

4. Have the ads rewritten or typed for the school bulletin board or for a special flyer to go out to the student body.

5. Organize a committee to go through the school or classroom lost and found to try to locate items using the ads as guides.

6. Repeat this activity at the end of the semester or just prior to seasonal breaks.

Nearly New

WHY: In conversation, the speaker and listener can interact in many ways (e.g., facial expression, gesture, tone, questioning) to ensure communication of a message. Since such interaction is seldom possible with written language, writing must be more detailed and descriptive than oral language. Describing and listing articles assembled for a charitable donation provides a concrete way to help children develop an awareness of the need for detail and description in written language.

WITH: Form for listing items, items in the home.

HOW: 1. On the form, the children list items in the home that are to be given to a charitable organization.

2. Help your child to be specific in her or his descriptions.

3. Help the child to determine the value of the items.

PARENT MINIPLAN

		Date____
Name _____		
Address_____		
Charitable Organization _____		

Item	Description	Value
	Total Value	

CHAPTER 2

The Purposes of Reading and Writing Are Many and Varied

The type of reading behavior we employ when we follow directions is very different from the type of reading behavior we employ when we read a light novel or newspaper. In a similar manner the types of composing or writing skills we use when writing a list differs from those we use in composing a formal letter of application or complaint. This variability of purpose, function and style is something children need to discover if they are to become literate in the broadest sense of the word.

Too frequently children develop the notion that reading is only what they do in their reading groups in school. They fail completely to see the relevance of this skill and activity to their lives or to realize that they use the skill repeatedly during the day. Children may also fail to develop flexible reading strategies unless classroom and home experiences provide an array of reading situations and adults help them to discover the different types of reading required in varying situations.

Ann Brown (1977) has proposed a useful system for categorizing reading situations. She refers to:

a. Reading for gist or meaning: the type of reading we do when we read narrative stories or the newspaper.

b. Reading for doing: the type of reading we do when following directions on a cake box or kit.

c. Reading for remembering: the type of reading that characterizes most school activities in the upper grades and beyond. This type of reading requires students to identify, organize and relate important aspects of information and to employ strategies that will enable them to demonstrate this understanding in some form.

For young children many concepts about print revolve around labels and words. Many of the activities in this chapter focus initially on a word level. The objective is to help children build on what they already know as a result of their real-world encounters with print. Teachers and parents should, however, keep in mind that reading involves much more than word identification.

In several activities, an instructional sequence is suggested which begins by having children use individual words to read, illustrate or write. This word is then used as the basis of a more elaborate piece of reading and/or writing. For example, in **I Can Read** (page 41), children find pictures of familiar products and label them. As the next step, they are encouraged to complete a key sentence, (*John can read "Sunshine Orange Juice."*). The activity could be further extended by writing or dictating about going to buy orange juice and why the family purchases a particular brand.

Children need to develop more than simple decoding skills. They need to develop an understanding that reading demands are situation-specific and that different strategies are needed in different situations. The following activities are designed to help illustrate some of the varying purposes of reading and writing.

READING LOG

WHY: Children frequently fail to see the functions reading serves in their lives. They sometimes think of reading as limited to the activity they do in groups in school. Reading logs can help children expand their notions of reading and raise their awareness of how frequently they use print.

WITH: Reading Log Booklet.

HOW: 1. Make a record booklet containing several pages of clean, lined paper.

2. Label the cover "Reading Log". Children might enjoy assembling the booklet and illustrating the cover.

3. Young children can use the booklet to list or dictate all the items they read both in and out of school. The list might include typical school terms, items in the grocery store, street signs, store names, and so on. Older children can list situations in which they typically read or need to read or would like to be able to read.

WHAT ELSE: 1. The words that younger children list can form the core of a "sight vocabulary" list.

2. Situations suggested by older children's logs may provide you with ideas for instructional activities certain to be meaningful and motivating to these children. For example, if a number of children indicated they would like to be able to read the directions for a popular board game, those directions can be the focus of many reading activities within the typical developmental reading program.

1. blackboard
2. cash register
3. school bus

Reading Log

WHY: Children frequently fail to see the functions reading serves in their lives. They sometimes think of reading as limited to the activity they do in groups in school. Reading logs can help children expand their notions of reading and raise their awareness of how frequently they use print in their everyday activities.

HOW: 1. Have the child fold an 8½″ x 11″ sheet of paper into thirds. Cut along folds. On one third, the child can design a cover. Then clip or staple all three pieces together at the top. On page one, have the child write or dictate the names of items around the house or in the neighborhood that she and he can read. On page two, the child writes or dictates the things she and he needs to read or would like to be able to read.

2. Encourage the child to notice how many words she or he can already read.

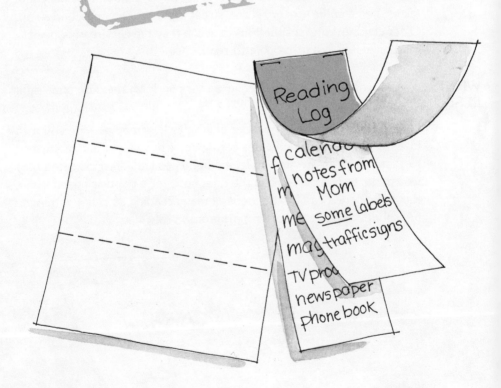

I CAN READ

WHY: In their world outside of school, children are often in situations where they encounter print (e.g., reading street signs, store names, labels, menus). As a result of these encounters, they acquire a core of functional words that relate to their everyday experiences. Teachers can point out that this type of experience is, indeed, reading and help children begin to think of themselves as successful readers.

WITH: Magazines, newspapers, catalogs, construction paper, scissors, paste.

HOW: 1. Have children locate pictures of items their family uses and they recognize from a file of local newspapers, magazines, and catalogs. They can be store names, food products, household cleaners, or toys.

2. Cut out the pictures that contain labels and paste them on individual sheets of construction paper.

3. As children complete the cutting and pasting, they read the labeling print to the teacher and she or he writes the following key sentence under the picture: "John can read _____." This enables children to see the meaningful print in its real-world context and in the teacher's print.

4. Have the children read the completed key sentences aloud.

WHAT ELSE: 1. **I Can Read** posters can become a bulletin board display.

2. The individual posters can be combined into a set of group books. Combine four or five pages and add a sheet which lists all the words in the group book. Be sure to have children read the books as part of an assignment or make them part of the classroom library available to be checked out.

3. Send home individual posters with instructions that children read the key sentences to their parents.

I CAN READ CARD SET

WHY: Real-world materials can be used for a variety of activities designed to develop reading skills and broaden the child's concept of reading.

WITH: Six index cards per set (The larger the basic card set you build, the more useful it will be.), felt-tip markers, glue, laminating materials, old magazines, labels and wrappers from familiar products.

HOW: 1. Collect four matching ads.

2. Cut the pictures of the product out of two of the ads and glue on separate index cards.

3. Cut the product's name out of the two remaining ads and glue on index cards.

4. Write the product's name on two cards.

WHAT ELSE: This card game is played following the same principle as in the card game "Go Fish". Players draw cards from a central pack, trying to build sets. The player with the highest number of sets when the central pack is exhausted is the winner.

> Level 1: Players match pictures to form sets.
> Level 2: Players match picture card with print card to form sets.
> Level 3: Players match print cards to form sets.

Magazine Search

WHY: One of the primary purposes of writing is to label. Children encounter labels (on food products and toys, for example) from a very young age. Because these items are encountered in meaningful situations, the child often learns to interpret these labels. It is likely that children use all the clues available on the label (e.g., pictures, color, stylized print) to make the interpretation. You can extend this interpretative behavior by focusing on the print aspect of labels in activities like the following.

HOW: 1. Have each family member locate a picture of a favorite dessert from a set of magazines or the Sunday newspaper.

2. Cut these out and paste the pictures on a sheet of paper. Be sure to include labeling print or have the person label the item (e.g., chocolate pie, Max's super cheese pie).

3. At the bottom of each sheet have the child complete the following key sentence:

> Dad's favorite dessert is _____.
> Mom's favorite dessert is _____.
> Gail's favorite dessert is _____.

Encourage the child to do as much of the writing as possible.

WHAT ELSE: 1. Post the sheets on the refrigerator and choose one person's favorite dessert each night. You can extend the writing aspect of the activity by suggesting the child write out a schedule for the week as such:

> *On Monday, we will have Dad's favorite—ice cream.*

Be sure to remind the child to use the sheets and calendar as a resource for spelling.

2. Combine the sheets into a booklet and be sure to have the child read "The Family Dessert Book" to important others, such as neighbors or grandparents.

3. Other themes can be developed in a similar way. Children will enjoy compiling a booklet of toys they would like to have, things they would like to do when they grow up, places they would like to visit.

WHO IS HERE TODAY?

WHY: An activity which is highly motivating for most children involves helping them learn to read and write their own name. Teachers can capitalize on children's enthusiasm for this personal accomplishment by involving them in an important aspect of classroom business—taking attendance. In addition to promoting recognition of their own and classmates' names, this activity helps children see the functional aspects of reading and writing.

WITH: A large pocket chart or bulletin board display on which the teacher has written each child's name. A name card for each child is cut in a familiar shape or figure. Yarn, colored paper, crayons, etc., to decorate the name-card figure.

HOW: 1. Write the name of each class member below one pocket or slot on a large poster. Attach to a bulletin board and title it "Who Is Here Today?" Prepare a name card for each child with her or his name printed on it.

2. On one of the first days of class, let each child personalize and decorate his or her name card. The children will probably enjoy an opportunity to show their name cards to one another. This sharing time is an excellent opportunity for children to *read* their own name to the group.

3. Put the name cards into a container at the end of each day. In the morning, children go to the container and each finds his or her name card. Each card is then posted in the appropriate slot or envelope.

4. You can then take attendance very quickly by glancing at the "Who Is Here Today?" poster.

WHAT ELSE: 1. This activity provides a natural lead-in to activities such as counting how many boys, girls, or people there are in the class or who is here or absent on a particular day.

2. As the year goes on, children can take a more active role in completing attendance forms for the office.

Who is Here Today?

Joe	John	Sue	Dana Cole	Jane
Joe Allen	John Brown	Sue Dunne	Dana Cole	Jane Johnson
Amy	Lisa	Mark	Joyce	
Amy Fritz	Tony Green	Lisa Hayes	Mark Jones	Joyce Clark
Andy	Sally	Michelle	Bob	Nina
Andy Klein	Sally Lewis	Michelle Lee	Bob Miller	Nina Nelson
Steve	Billy	Karen	Sandy	Bobby
Steve Noble	Billy Potts	Karen Rogers	Sandy Smith	Bobby White

Who is Here Today?
How many boys are here?
How many girls are here?
How many children are here?

Name Tags   Number Cards

Name That Place

WHY: Reading her or his own name is a beginning reading activity that almost all children find motivating. You can capitalize on this interest and extend it by using name cards at home.

HOW: 1. Prepare a name card for each family member, using her or his familiar name (e.g., Mom, Daddy, Gail, Davey). Use a folded 3″ x 5″ card or lightweight posterboard so that you can use the name cards many times.

2. Use these cards to assign (or reassign) places at the table. At first you might want to place the cards at each family member's usual seat. At another meal, or on another day, have family members take different seats according to where each name card is placed. As your children become familiar with reading all the names, they will enjoy "assigning" places with the name cards.

WHEN DO I?

WHY: One of the great advantages of written language is that it can serve as a record for memory. Even young children can benefit from this advantage as they learn to manage, organize and plan their classroom day.

WITH: A large poster with key pictures or drawings and accompanying print that notes the regularly scheduled major activities in the classroom day.

HOW: 1. During meeting or a classroom planning session, review with the children the daily regular schedule your class will follow.

2. List these major activities along with the time for each (e.g., 9:00-9:10 Opening; 9:10-9:45 Choice Time; 9:45-10:45 Reading) on a poster or the chalkboard. A clock face with the hands positioned at the time specified may be helpful. Especially at the beginning of the year, you will probably have to have a key picture or drawing for each activity listed. Children enjoy helping you find or make these.

When do I?

9:00-9:15 Class Meeting

9:15-9:45 Choice Time

9:45-10:15 Name Tags

10:15-10:45 Snack Time

10:45-11:30 Play Time

11:30-11:45 Clean Up

Tube Time

WHY: Even young children will recognize the value of a written schedule in organizing their day if the schedule relates to something that is personally meaningful. This activity will help children develop a way to deal with the highly abstract concept of time in a way that is meaningful and concrete. In addition, children will practice reading in real-world situations, using reading materials, such as the television guide, that are motivating and familiar.

HOW: 1. Talk with your child about the amount of time available for television viewing.

2. When you agree on a set amount of time for the week, use the newspaper or other commercially available weekly guide to select the shows the child will watch during the week.

3. Help the child make a chart or list that includes the names of the shows, the channel, the time for each show, and a running total of the time for the week. (With a young child, you will probably want to make a daily chart without the running total.)

An additional benefit of this preplanning may be increased selectivity by the child as she or he chooses which shows to watch. You can encourage this and draw attention to specials or particular shows you might prefer to have your child watch.

WHAT ELSE: 1. Use a rating sheet for the shows selected to encourage the child to think about aspects of the program which make the particular show entertaining: characters, story line, use of humor.

Show Title:		
Rater:		Length:
Interesting ☐	Funny ☐	Boring ☐

2. This same kind of planning will be very helpful to children in budgeting time for other after school activities and homework. Many children simply don't know where to begin when they are first confronted with homework, particularly long-range assignments. Planning to do the work in reasonable chunks over a period of time and using a written schedule can make a big difference.

Day	Show	Channel	Time	# Minutes
Monday				
Tuesday				
Wednesday				
Thursday				
Friday				
Saturday				
Sunday				
Total Number of Minutes				

TV TIME

LEND A HAND

WHY: It is far easier to keep track of schedules or reminders when they are written down. Children are often expected to participate in classroom schedules. Providing schedules or reminders with picture clues along with labeling print will demonstrate the usefulness of writing to help in organizing the classroom day.

WITH: A large pocket chart or slotted poster. Pictures gathered from old magazines. Tag or lightweight posterboard job cards or job card necklaces (see illustration). Yarn, felt-tip pens and crayons.

HOW: 1. Discuss with the children the kinds of classroom housekeeping jobs that need to be done on a regular basis.

2. Have them help you find pictures or draw pictures that represent these classroom jobs.

3. Together, decide on an appropriate name or title for each task. Write these on the board and go over them with the class.

4. Post each job title on a large pocket chart or slotted poster. Then prepare a matching job card. (For young children, you could attach yarn at each end to make a job necklace.)

5. At the beginning of each day, you can assign a child to each job by distributing the job card or necklaces. At the end of the day, children return the card or necklace to the proper slot or pocket by matching the job name on the card or necklace with the job name under the appropriate pocket or slot.

WHAT ELSE: When you first begin this activity, be sure to reread the task names or titles as *you* assign jobs. Continue to do this until children can read the task names independently. As you think they can do this, call a job name and let a child go and get the appropriate card or necklace.

At the beginning of the year, wearing the card or necklace will be very helpful to the teacher and other students in monitoring who is responsible for particular tasks each day.

As children become more familiar with classroom routine and responsibilities, this system can be modified in a number of ways:

1. You can assign tasks by placing children's name cards in particular job pockets or slots.

2. Children can select jobs of their choice by signing up on a special job sign-up sheet.

3. Job assignments can be made for longer periods of time by posting a weekly job schedule.

4. When job cards or necklaces are no longer necessary, you can assign or select particular classroom jobs by placing a name card or marker (e.g., a clip with the child's name) in the pocket or slot.

Many Hands/Light Work

WHY: Many people find it easier to keep track of schedules and reminders when they are written down. Providing a job chart with picture clues and labeling print is a way of demonstrating the particular usefulness of writing in this situation and will make it easier for you and your child to monitor his or her responsibilities in your home.

HOW: 1. Discuss with your family the kinds of household tasks you would like them to share.

2. Write them down and go over the list with each child, making sure she or he can see the print as you write and read.

3. On a large piece of paper or cardboard, list the names or titles of those tasks with which each child will help—making bed, straightening room, mealtime cleanup. Attach to refrigerator. Mark each child's name on a clip-type clothespin (or use a name card attached to a paper clip). Clip the pin next to a job to indicate which job a child is responsible for that day. As time goes by, you and your child may want to assign jobs for a longer period of time.

WHAT ELSE: Check sheets can be developed and kept next to the job charts and jobs can be checked when completed.

DAY BY DAY

WHY: For many adults, a personal calendar is filled with notes and reminders of appointments, special events, things to do or buy. Including this type of information on the classroom calendar will increase students' contact with meaningful print and at the same time will give them concrete references as they learn to organize days, weeks, and months. This meaningful recording of events also makes the very abstract concepts of time and space more concrete for young children.

WITH: Monthly calendar sheets with spaces large enough for notes.

HOW: 1. As you do your daily calendar work, note special things that are happening in the classroom (e.g., a special visitor, the first day of snow, John's turn to rotate the eggs in the incubator).

2. At the end of each week, you and/or the children go over the week's notations.

3. Keep these monthly calendar sheets on a chart rack so that children can look at past months from time to time. They will enjoy rereading about the special things that have taken place.

WHAT ELSE: 1. A nice way to start this activity each month is to note holidays or class members' birthdays which will occur during the month.

2. Children can make a list of things they have done each day or week to let parents know what is happening in school. The calendar can be used as a reference for making a list to send home in a weekly newsletter (e.g., *This Week in Room 22*).

OCTOBER

SUNDAY	MONDAY	TUESDAY	WEDNESDAY	THURSDAY	FRIDAY	SATURDAY
	1	2	3 Amy's Birthday	4 Visitors' Day	5 ✓	6 ✓
7 ✓	8 trip to town library	9 ✓	10 Movie! ✓	11 ✓	12 Columbus Day ✓	13 ✓
14 ✓	15 Leaves starting to turn	16 Johnny's Birthday	17	18	19	20 Football Game
21	22	23	24	25 Nature Walk	26	27
28	29 . Bring in Leaves	30	31 Halloween Parade			

The Nicest Thing That Happened Today

WHY: You can help your child recognize the value of written language as a way to record and preserve experiences and events. In addition, you can help your child develop and refine the concept of time by using the calendar in a way that measures time in relation to daily experiences.

HOW: 1. Use either a diary type calendar or monthly calendar sheets with blocks large enough to write in notes.

2. Shortly before bedtime, talk with the child about the nicest things that happened during the day. Then let the child choose one event to write about or dictate for that day's calendar entry.

3. Make it a habit to review past days and weeks. You and your child will enjoy rereading and recalling the pleasant events you have recorded.

WHAT ELSE: 1. You and/or the child can make personalized monthly calendar sheets. Making her or his own provides extra practice in reading and writing the names of the days of the week and the month and becoming familiar with the sequence of days and months.

2. Books based on days of the week or months of the year, such as *Chicken Soup With Rice*, by Maurice Sendak, can be used to reinforce these terms and their sequence.

CHOICE TIME SELECTION

WHY: Frequently used words from the classroom environment and schedule are very appropriate choices to be included in the young readers' sight vocabulary. Providing numerous and active opportunities which require children to deal with these words in print will help accomplish this goal.

WITH: A chart or poster which lists the activities or centers available in the classroom for those times when the children make their own selections, for example:

I will work at the listening center.
I will work at the writing center.
I will play math games.

Each sentence should be accompanied by a key picture which serves as an additional cue, especially when first using the chart.

HOW: 1. Children should come to the meeting area in small groups.

2. Have each child select, then identify, the activity or center in which she or he plans to work. At first children may simply point to a picture to specify their choice. To develop this as a reading activity, you can point out the accompanying sentence when you feel the children are ready.

3. Read accompanying sentences to the child, having the child read along.

4. When the children have progressed in reading they can read the print independently to indicate their choice time selection.

WHAT ELSE: 1. Children will enjoy helping locate or draw key pictures for the chart.

2. You and the children will probably want to modify or expand the activities as time goes by.

3. It may take quite a while for children to use the print on the chart independently, but once they can, the activity can be extended by preparing sentence strips which duplicate those on the chart but without the key pictures. Have children indicate their choice time selection using the sentence strips. They can check their own reading by matching the sentence strip to the sentence on the chart.

CHOICE TIME ACTIVITIES

I will work in the listening center.

I will work at the writing center.

I will work at the workbench.

I will practice math facts.

I will work in the art center.

I will read with a buddy.

I will play word bingo.

I will go to the library.

Snack Time Sweepstakes

WHY: It is usually easier to read about things that are familiar and of interest. Therefore, commonly used words from the environment are most appropriate for including in the beginning reader's sight vocabulary. Make lists of frequently used words, and use the lists to provide functional practice in reading and writing. For example, have the child rely on a list of foods when he or she selects a snack.

HOW: 1. With your child, make a list of the fruits, vegetables, nuts, cereals, crackers, and cheeses the child enjoys as an after-school snack. You might want to spice up the list with some interesting combinations, such as "ants on a log" (celery sticks filled with peanut butter and topped off with raisins).

2. Reread the list several times, inviting the child to read along with you. Point to or frame the words as you read them.

3. Have the child choose seven or eight favorites and write those on duplicate word cards. (You may need to adjust the size of the word card depending on the skill of the writer.) Children may want to find or draw an appropriate picture for the word cards as well.

4. Assemble the seven or eight snack items. Fasten one of the duplicate word cards to each item. Put the second set in a large bowl or hat. Then put the snack items in a special place accessible to the child.

5. Each day after school, the child chooses one of the word cards which will be the snack for the day. Matching the word card to its duplicate on the snack items list provides an independent, self-check system for the child.

WHAT ELSE: 1. If several family members participate, there will be much more variety in eating as well as reading and writing.

2. If the family enjoys the activity, it could be used for scheduling and selecting other meals (e.g., *Breakfast Grab Bag*) or other types of activities such as day trip destinations.

3. A way in which to follow up and extend reading and writing opportunities is to make the day's snack an entry on the weekly or monthly calendar sheet, such as:

Monday's snack was peanut butter and banana on graham crackers. Today I tried raw peas.

DO YOU READ ME?

WHY: The controlling aspect of written language may be familiar to children from experience with traffic signs or other written directions, such as: **Keep Out**; **Do Not Disturb**; **Keep Off the Grass**. Print can be used to regulate aspects of the classroom environment in a similar manner.

WITH: Felt-tip markers, tagboard sentence strips.

HOW: 1. In discussions with the class, generate the standards for behavior to which all class members must subscribe.

2. Write these on a chart and post them as public criteria for behavior.

3. If and when a child needs to be reminded about standards, she or he can be referred to the posted standards, "Remember #3."

> ## NO RUNNING IN THE HALL

WHAT ELSE: 1. Posted standards, directions, or rules of behavior are also appropriate for use of centers or special equipment, such as:

> ## ONLY 3 PEOPLE IN THE PLAYHOUSE

2. Children can make individual directives on tagboard strips, such as:

> ## DO NOT WRECK THIS BLOCK STRUCTURE

3. Sign-up sheets for various activities and centers will help organize the classroom while providing a practical opportunity to practice reading and writing. Children who want to use a particular area need to find the correct day and sign their name. They need to use reading skills to find which day they paint and with which children.

Replenishing the Shelves

WHY: One of the important functions of writing is that it can serve as a record for memory. We can save time and energy by writing down frequently used phone numbers or directions to new destinations. We can shop more efficiently with a list of needed items. The more opportunities children have to participate in making and using lists, the more directly they will appreciate and value this very practical function of written language.

WITH: Use a magnetic clip or tape to post a master shopping list to the refrigerator door. Be sure to keep a supply of pencils nearby. (You might want to keep a pencil attached.) Family members note items that have run out or items they need.

HOW: 1. Encourage making lists in other appropriate situations: holiday cards and gifts, items needed for camping trips, school supplies.

2. Use sign-up lists for the day each week when particular family members have priority in using high-demand items: a special record, a favorite game, the right to choose which television show everyone watches at 8 p.m.

Birthday Club
Membership Form

Name: _____

Date of Birth: _____

Age: _____

Class: _____

_____
Signature of Applicant

_____
Signature of Teacher

Birthday Club
Membership Card

Name: _____

Birth Date: _____

MAKING IT IN THE REAL WORLD:
Filling Out Applications and Forms

WHY: Even young children can recognize the importance of being able to complete forms which require information in a prescribed manner.

WITH: Application forms you have designed.

HOW: 1. Develop a club theme which rewards children for successful completion of an application blank. For example, a class birthday club might have a birthday crown and a special privilege for the birthday person upon successful completion of the *Birthday Club Membership Form.*

2. Design a simple club application asking for information such as name, address, birthdate, school, and so on.

3. Children complete application forms after appropriate prior practice.

WHAT ELSE: 1. Computer response sheets used for many standardized tests are often confusing for children. In the weeks prior to testing, use old sheets and provide several practice sessions using them.

2. Once children are familiar with classroom routine and the daily classroom housekeeping tasks, encourage them to "apply" for the ones they enjoy and feel they could do best. Have the children apply for classroom jobs by completing an application form.

Name: _____

Job: _____

Why I would be good:

_____

_____

_____

3. Have the children involved in the routine administrative tasks of the classroom, such as filling in the attendance sheet and taking the milk count. Children can take turns being recorders for the day. If your school doesn't use forms for this, you can make them yourself.

PARENT MINIPLAN

Sign on the Dotted Line

WHY: Even young children can recognize the importance of being able to complete forms which require information in a prescribed manner. Learning their name and address are major tasks for young children. You can make this task more meaningful for your child and help develop an important functional skill at the same time by utilizing the many application forms designed for children at fast-food restaurants and other commercial establishments.

HOW: 1. Many stores and restaurants have club plans that children can participate in by successfully completing a simple application. The birthday ice-cream cone or free soft drink with a food purchase are excellent motivations to successfully complete the the form.

2. Public library cards can usually be obtained when a child can complete a simple application. This activity has a double payoff as it encourages reading of the library literature.

3. Many fast-food establishments have service evaluation forms. These provide a good extension of this type of activity.

4. Some contest forms available in grocery stores or mailed to homes could be completed by children. If postage is prepaid, why not let your child submit them. The possibility of winning a contest certainly motivates a child to complete forms.

STOP THE ACTION

WHY: All of us have had children who read words orally without understanding or thinking about what they mean. This reading behavior sometimes results from instructional practices that stress decoding at the expense of meaning. **Stop the Action** stresses the meaning of the word rather than its pronunciation. Children will enjoy this "active" reading as a transitional activity.

WITH: Chalkboard, word cards, craft sticks.

HOW: 1. Have the children brainstorm a group of words for things they like to do: run, jump, jog, skip, hop. Write the words from the brainstorming session on the chalkboard.

2. After reviewing them several times, select a set of ten and write the words on individual tag cards. Attach the word cards to craft sticks and add a "Stop" sign.

3. Hold up one card at a time. All the players do what the word card says until the leader holds up the stop sign.

WHAT ELSE: Expand the set of word cards or change them (e.g., things we do in the summer or winter; things we do when we are happy, sad). Since these words will become part of the child's sight vocabulary, they will be excellent to use as you work on word analysis and vocabulary activities.

Song Board Toss

WHY: Sometimes beginning readers become almost too concerned with the pronunciation aspect of reading. This action oriented reading activity emphasis the meaning of the words rather than translation from print to the oral representation.

HOW: 1. Use an 11″ x 14″ sheet of posterboard to make the song board. (These sheets are available in many supermarkets.) Use a felt-tip pen or crayon to divide the poster into four boxes.

2. Write the names of four familiar songs on 3″ x 5″ cards.

3. Fasten one card in each box using double stick tape so you can change the song titles or use the board for another category by changing the 3″ x 5″ cards.

4. Have the child toss a coin or bean bag onto the board, then sing the song on which it lands.

WHAT ELSE: 1. Increasing the number of boxes increases the difficulty of the activity. If your children enjoy the challenge, do it

2. Use the activity with several family members or friends taking turns. When everyone is familiar with all the song titles, the group sings each song as the bean bag lands on it.

3. Boards can be used for other choice activities—fillings for sandwiches at lunchtime or making decisions about who takes a bath first.

CHAPTER 3
Written Language and Spoken Language Differ in Characteristics and Purposes Served

Written language differs from spoken language in some major ways. These differences contribute to the difficulty children have in mastering written language.

- Written language is more elaborate—there is a need to make things more explicit because the reader does not share the context with the writer and cannot signal the need for clarification.
- In recording information the writer addresses an absent audience. The writer knows nothing about the reader's background information or interest. The writer must take on the role of the reader and fill in needed information.
- Written language communicates information over time and space. It serves the purposes of communicating with people who are not immediately present and of leaving records over time.

Writing provides a unique opportunity for the development of the idea of an absent audience and therefore the need to make events, situations, and motives explicit in language. This notion of explicitness must be learned by young writers. Children learn to speak in an environment that provides a wide variety of clues to meanings, such as facial expressions and gestures, in addition to spoken language. Picture the fourteen-month-old who points to the cookie jar and utters one word. In doing this, the young individual expresses a complex message in that one word, a message that identifies what she or he wants, the person who will get it for her or him, and the recipient of the action. The six-year-old telling about school is no less context bound.

Written language, on the other hand, requires that things be stated explicitly. There can be no assumption that the reader has any knowledge of the circumstances or event being communicated by print. (In writing, children often leave big gaps in the action assuming the reader can "fill in" these gaps.) Developing command of this elaborative nature of written language is a lifelong task. Young children are at a particular disadvantage because they are unaware of the information needed by the other person. In children's oral language communication, the context fills in the information that they leave out. Young children, therefore, have little awareness of the need to elaborate via language.

Helping children understand the characteristics of written language and the purposes best served by written communication is a necessary foundation for literacy. Children need to experience situations where the needs of the receiver of their message can be made explicit to them. They need to experience functional situations where leaving written messages is more convenient than oral communication. They also need to encounter situations where making records of events to span time serves an important purpose in their lives. This awareness must be discovered by the child, but structuring by the adult is necessary to help the child see the information that others need in order to understand the message.

STEP BY STEP: Writing Directions

WHY: Understanding that one function of writing is to communicate information to others who are not with you at the moment, and that the information must be clearly communicated in words, is not immediately apparent to young children. Creating situations where children have to describe how to do things and have concrete ways of testing the effectiveness of their ideas does much to foster this understanding.

WITH: Whatever materials necessary for children to demonstrate their favorite activity, paper, pencil.

HOW: 1. A child demonstrates a favorite activity or skill, such as building a model airplane or making a paper mask.

2. While the child works, you record the steps and directions, using the *child's* exact language.

3. Read back to the child, allowing the child to make changes. Rewrite* and revise as much as the child feels is necessary. If this activity is carried out with a group, the group can be helpful in clarifying and checking sequence.

4. Give the directions to someone not present at the demonstration to see whether she or he can successfully do the activity by following the steps.

*One advantage of written language is that it provides a record which can be reused and rewritten. Since children are naturally egocentric, it provides a good way to help them become aware of the perspective of others.

Hide 'n' Seek Snack

WHY: Written directions must be clear and concise in order to be followed correctly. An activity such as **Hide 'n' Seek Snack** provides an opportunity for the child to discover, firsthand, the need for precision in this type of writing.

HOW: 1. Choose a place to hide the child's after-school snack.

2. Write directions for the child to use to "seek" the snack. Keep the directions simple the first few times you try this activity, and try to include some humor or an element of novelty. For example, the directions might be in rhyme.

> In the dining room,
>   under Dot's seat
> You'll find a snack
>   that's good to eat!

Or, the directions might employ a play on words.

> Don't monkey around!
> You can find your snack
> In "a plain yellow wrapper"
> In a basket on the counter.

3. Be sure to run through the directions to catch any mistakes before leaving them for your child.

4. After your child has located the snack, discuss the activity and try to identify what made it easy or difficult to follow the directions.

WHAT ELSE: 1. Eric Carle's *The Secret Birthday Message* is the story of a child who successfully follows a series of clues to find a birthday gift. You and your child might enjoy reading this book together before you try this activity.

2. You might want to write a "secret birthday message" for your child. Write a numbered series of directions or clues and place them strategically around the house. The child will be able to tell that she or he is on the right track so long as the numbers are in sequence. The search will be even more fun if the route is circuitous. Use your imagination in writing the directions. For example, after successfully arriving at the destination in Clue #1, the child might find a second clue which reads, "You're getting warm; now go to the freezer."

3. After your child has used your written directions several times, she or he might enjoy turning tables and writing directions which lead other family members to a snack or treat.

ORIENTEERING

WHY: Precision is a characteristic of written directions. Vagueness on the writer's part will result in directions that cannot be followed by the reader. Learning to use a compass and follow written instructions can help children discover the importance of clear directions. After a little practice, children can try writing their own directions and have their classmates try them out to see how well they work.

WITH: Compass, directional clue cards, reward.

HOW: 1. Organize the class into small work groups of three or four students and discuss terms used in orienteering.

2. Give each group of students a compass and begin to familiarize them with reading it. Give verbal directions and practice in "pacing off".

3. Develop a course using a compass for the students to read and follow. Use the school grounds to develop your course, for example:
   - a. Start at the flagpole.
   - b. Go north 10 steps.
   - c. Go east 25 steps.
   - d. Are you facing the big oak tree?

4. Give each group of students the first directional clue card for the course.

5. Have the succeeding directions posted at each destination point so that as the students read and proceed, they will then find the next direction card. Give the number of paces and direction for each card.

6. Directions for a special activity, such as an extra 10-minute outdoor playtime or some other treat at the end of the course, will enhance the children's sense of accomplishment.

WHAT ELSE: With experience, students can write their own directions for their classmates to follow. Classmates can evaluate the clarity of directions on a feedback sheet.

a. Start at the flagpole.

b. Go north 10 steps.

c. Go east 25 steps.

d. Are you facing the big oak tree?

e. Look for the next direction card.

The Way to Our House

WHY: Writing directions will give children practice in a type of writing that requires precision and clarity. Vagueness on their part will result in directions that cannot be followed by others. Preparing a map and a set of written directions to your house can promote awareness of the need for clear and explicit language.

HOW: 1. Use city, town or county maps to develop a map of your immediate neighborhood to direct people to your house.

2. Work with your child to develop a set of written directions to accompany the map. Your directions might start from a nearby busy intersection or other landmark.

3. After a shopping trip or outing, have the child act as navigator, and using the map and directions guide your trip home. After the trial run, make any revisions you both think will improve the directions.

4. Duplicate your map and directions to use as needed.

WHAT ELSE: You might want to make an enlarged insert of your street for the youngest members of the family.

TREASURE HUNT

WHY: Children are used to adults telling and demonstrating. One important characteristic of written language is that it can provide the needed information when someone is not available to *show* or *tell*. The **Treasure Hunt** activity creates a need for the children to obtain information which is available only in written form.

WITH: Treasure map, direction strips, confirming cards.

HOW: 1. Develop a map for your class of an important area of the school. For children with little experience in map reading, you will probably want to start with a familiar and relatively small area such as your classroom. As the children develop skill in using maps, you can add additional areas.

2. Have a key for using the map. Discuss the key with the class. For example:

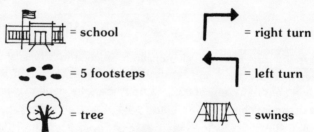

3. Divide the class into teams of four or five members.

4. Develop a set of directions cards for each group of children to use along with the map to find the hidden treasure.

- You can reuse the map and adjust the difficulty of the directions as the children become more skillful in using the map.

- The directions should be written so that children need to refer to the map to progress in their search for the treasure. For example, use terms from the map key in your written directions, "Start

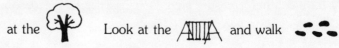

- Each team member will be responsible for completing directions on one of the strips. You will need to work through a sample set of directions to be sure the children understand the teamwork that will be necessary to successfully find the hidden treasure.

5. In order to assure the children that they are on course, a card could be placed at each step on the route confirming that they have correctly followed the previous direction.

> *This completes direction #3.*
>
> *Now go on to direction #4.*

6. Have a prize as the treasure—candy, one free homework ticket per team member, one free extra recess ticket per team member. Record the time to complete the hunt for each team.

7. Have each team (...) .s its venture to find the treasure. Try to draw out the problem directions. Discuss how it is often difficult to follow written directions because you misinterpret the direction.

WHAT ELSE:
1. Each team might try to improve its set of directions by making them more specific. Now, exchange sets of directions and try to have another Treasure Hunt Day.

2. Make a graph of each team's time for the first hunt and again for the second hunt. Does experience with following written directions improve team performance?

3. Each team might want to develop a new treasure map with new directions. You will have to check out each map for accuracy before you have another Treasure Hunt Day. Discuss and record the results of this hunt.

Muffin Map

WHY: Reading directions is different from reading a story, but both are important and both require practice to gain proficiency. The type of activity suggested in **Muffin Map** requires the type of reading where attention to detail and sequence is important. When practice includes games and family projects, mastering new skills will be natural and easy.

HOW: 1. Write a set of directions for accomplishing a specific activity, such as finding a new book hidden somewhere in the house, visiting a neighbor or friend, or taking a trip to the zoo. (Try out the directions before continuing with this activity so you are sure everything works.)

2. Cut slips of paper and write one direction on each piece. Number the slips in sequence for accomplishing this activity.

3. Prepare muffin or cupcake mix, pouring the batter into muffin tins.

4. Place one slip of paper into each muffin. Bake.

5. Distribute to member of the family (and friends) all muffins containing the directions.

6. They must use the numbers to determine where their part of the directions fit into the sequence. Once the sequence is established, everyone will be able to enjoy the activity.

SCAVENGER HUNT

WHY: This activity helps students recognize the need for precision when writing instructions for others to follow.

WITH: Scavenger lists, paper bags.

HOW: 1. Make up lists of items to be searched for by teams of four or five students. Items might include:

2" pencil with eraser	comb
school box	bobbie pin
white shoestring	apple slice
blue barrett	brown sock with stripes

2. Divide the class into groups and give each group a list containing a different set of items along with a bag or other container in which to place the items each group finds. Be sure to provide time for each group to preview its list and clarify questions, if there are any.

3. Specify the time available and how you will signal that time is up. Be sure to note the space or areas available for the scavenger hunt. This is especially important if students will be going outside the classroom.

4. Record the time the teams begin. As each team returns, note when it finished.

5. Check the items brought in against the group's list.

6. Discuss any difficulties encountered.

7. Determine the winner based on number of items found in the least amount of time.

WHAT ELSE: 1. Save the lists to be exchanged and used another time.

2. Have the students make up a scavenger list for another classroom and organize a scavenger hunt—complete with written directions—for those children.

3. Help the students make up a list of items in the school "Lost and Found". Point out the need for specifics, such as color, size, brand labels,

if available, so that readers can identify their particular belongings from a written description. Duplicate the list for each classroom. Classroom teachers can post the list so that students (and parents) can check for lost items.

4. At times you may want to have all the items for a scavenger hunt relate to a particular theme or unit of study (signs of fall or spring, tools used by pioneers, toys unique to the 1980s).

Library Return

WHY: Many times a list can help us organize and complete a task more successfully than if we trust our memories. Creating a memory record is a very important function of written language. By helping your child participate in list making, you emphasize this function.

HOW: 1. Visiting the library is one activity that is often done by a family together on the weekend. It can be very confusing to remember to return everyone's books.

2. Use a chart to record the titles of the books checked out by each family member. Your child can help you enter the titles next to the name of each person.

3. On library return day, each family member can refer to the list to make sure she or he has gathered up all the books that need to be returned.

4. Post the list on the message center in your home.

WHAT ELSE: 1. Saturday errands can be many and varied. Make a list of all those things that the family wants to accomplish on Saturday.

2. A parent who travels often could enlist the help of his or her child in making a packing checklist, then checking off items as they are packed.

3. Items to be taken to the dry cleaners could be listed as they are gathered together.

JAM SESSION

WHY: Different types of writing require different types of reading. When reading for pleasure (e.g., a novel or newspaper), one reads for important ideas or gist of a message. In other situations (e.g., studying a text), one must read more precisely and attend more carefully to aspects of the writing, such as details and sequence. Cooking activities often provide situations in which even younger children will see the need for precision in certain types of reading.

WITH: Recipe, ingredients and utensils, bread, butter, spreaders, napkins.

HOW: 1. Make copies of the strawberry jam recipe.

2. Read the recipe with the children and collect the ingredients and cooking utensils.

3. Help the children follow the instructions in the recipe.

4. Refrigerate the jam for a jam party the next day.

5. Give the children the responsibility of bringing the bread and butter for the jam party.

STRAWBERRY JAM
(Refrigerator-Freezer Type)

| 4 cups of sugar | 3/4 cup of water |
| 2 cups of crushed ripe strawberries (about 2 pints) | 1 box (1 3/4 ounces) powdered fruit pectin |

1. Add sugar to crushed strawberries in a large bowl; mix well and set aside.

2. Combine the water and pectin in a small saucepan; blend well. Bring to a boil for 1 minute, stirring constantly. Stir into sweetened strawberries. Continue stirring about 3 minutes. (There will be some sugar crystals remaining.)

3. Ladle jam into clean, hot jars, seal immediately, and set aside until jam is set, 24 to 48 hours.

4. Store in refrigerator to use within 2 or 3 weeks. Store in freezer if kept longer.

Yield: 5 half-pints jam.

"Strawberry Jam" from the **Canning and Freezing Book,** by D. Munston, The Culinary Arts Institute, Chicago, Ill, 1975.

WHAT ELSE: 1. You can further develop the students' notion of the uses of writing by making lists of ingredients and writing invitations as part of this activity.

2. *Recipes for Learning* by Gail Lewis and Jean Shaw is a good resource for a teacher interested in using cooking in the classroom (see Bibliography).

3. Collect children's favorite, tried and true recipes for a recipe book. Titles might be "Things I Like" or "Try It, You'll Like It."

Cold Drink Stand

WHY: Cooking activities help children develop an appreciation for the need to read directions in a particular sequence.

HOW: 1. Children prepare a pitcher of a favorite cold drink from a package or frozen concentrate, following directions on the label.

2. Drinks can be shared or "sold" to family members and friends.

WHAT ELSE: 1. Children may enjoy setting up a more elaborate stand. They will need to collect cups, a table, napkins, chairs. An attractive poster will help advertise the cold drink.

2. If children become involved in selling the cold drinks, other activities, such as keeping records of expenses and profits will follow naturally.

A ME BOOK

WHY: Children can recognize the value and function of written language in keeping records in a situation where the record documents personal data.

WITH: Information sheet, construction paper, picture file, paste, scissors, pencil.

HOW: 1. Prepare an information sheet for each child to fill out.

2. Have the children assemble a picture file (photos, pictures from magazines or illustrations) to use along with their written responses.

3. Identify and label each picture.

4. Have the child complete the information sheet by filling in written responses.

5. Each child can assemble a construction paper album or "Me" book. The child might enjoy illustrating the cover and creating a more personal or elaborate title.

WHAT ELSE: 1. Display the booklets and encourage children to read one another's by making this reading part of instructional activities or by making the booklets part of the classroom library, available to be checked out.

2. Let children interview each other with information sheets.

3. Assemble a class book of one or several of the sheets; for example, each child's response to the favorite foods or what they would like to be.

4. Encourage the child to develop her or his picture card caption response into a more elaborate story.

Growing Book

WHY: Children will appreciate the value of written language in preserving experiences over time when the record documents their own personal history. In this very meaningful context, the need for precision and accuracy in keeping records will be apparent.

HOW: 1. Help the child assemble four or five significant photos which trace her or his development, beginning with the earliest photo you have available. If this is not possible, you and the child can illustrate several important occasions (birthdays, holidays, family celebrations).

2. Identify and date each picture as accurately as possible.

3. Talk about each picture with your child; discuss the occasion in the photo and related events. Children enjoy hearing stories of "when they were babies" or of events they were too young to remember. It is likely you will both enjoy comparing memories or reactions to memories you share.

4. Have the child write or dictate a caption for each picture. These captions can be one word or may be a detailed retelling of the event in the photo. Children sometimes enjoy writing a brief caption independently, then writing or dictating a more comprehensive version with some help.

5. Reread the captions with your child several times and let the child reread or retell them.

6. Assemble a construction-paper album or **Growing Book**. The child might enjoy illustrating the cover and creating a more personal title for this book.

7. Encourage the child to share the book and reread it to other family members.

WHAT ELSE: 1. Some children want to write rather long and elaborate captions but lack the skill to do so independently. A way to enable children to do this more complex writing is to act as a secretary for initial dictation, then let the child recopy his or her story. The child gets many opportunities to practice both reading and writing in this sequence.

2. If the child's interest in the growing book persists and she or he is able to read it independently, encourage him or her to bring it to school to share with the teacher and other class members.

TIME CAPSULE

WHY: Written language bridges the gap between time and space. This unique characteristic can be made apparent to students in a concrete manner by having the class create a "time capsule".

WITH: Items to bury, box, shovel.

HOW: 1. Lay the foundation for this activity by reading or talking about the way archaeologists learn about past cultures through artifacts.

2. Have the class brainstorm a list of items they feel represent their lifestyle. One of the students or you should record the list of items.

3. Duplicate the list or prepare a form for class members to use to survey parents and friends. The survey results can be used to refine the list of items you select for the time capsule.

4. Collect the items and write a brief description of each. Re sure to explain the item's usefulness and importance to our current way of life.

5. Pack all the items and the written records in a box. Bury them for future generations to uncover.

WHAT ELSE: If the children will be going on to another class in the same school, arrange with their next year's teacher to retrieve the box.

Reminiscing

WHY: Children can discover that written records serve an important function as a link between past, present and future. Family records provide a tie to the past. By interviewing the oldest members of the family, children can learn information that might have been lost otherwise. Such information about events, relationships, reactions to historical and/or political events will give your child perspective and background for studying the past (particularly the time period recalled by her or his own relatives). Participation in this type of activity can be a pleasant experience for your child as she or he gets to know an older relative in a new way. It is likely the entire family will enjoy records—for the present and perhaps even more as time goes by.

HOW: 1. Help the child develop a set of questions for interviewing an older relative so that she or he will be sure to get information about important people and events in her or his family. Have the child practice several times so that she or he is very familiar with the questions and can be informal during the interview. (You will find a simple interview included, but will probably want to modify it or perhaps develop your own.)

2. Interview grandparents, great grandparents, aunts, uncles or others to document your personal family history. Tape the interviews, then write up selected facts contributed by different family members. Be sure to date and title tapes. They can be replayed and enjoyed from time to time.

Reminiscing Interview
(Sample Questions)

Person Interviewed: _____

Interview Conducted By: _____

1. Where were you born?

2. What were your parent's names? Where did they come from?

3. How many brothers and sisters do you have? What are their names? When were they born?

4. What things do you remember about your home life when you were a child? Where did you live?

5. How did your mother cook? What kind of stove was used?

6. What job did your dad have?

7. What was school like for you?

8. What things did you and your family do for fun?

9. Tell an interesting story from your past that you would like your future relatives to hear and enjoy.

TIME LINE

WHY: When the purpose for writing is obvious and the subject is interesting, children discover writing as meaningful and functional in their lives. Research projects, such as the one reflected in **Time Line**, help children record information in structured but functional ways. Through this activity children will find that recorded information, ordered on a time line, serves to provide a reference to the past and easier access for researching historical event.

WITH: Reference materials, a long roll of paper for the time line, record forms.

HOW: 1. As an action research activity related to a social studies project or study of your local or regional history, plan to visit school or local libraries, the city or town hall offices and museums where pertinent information can be found.

2. With the students, plan a note-taking format for the information they collect.

Date:_____

Event:_____

Significance:_____

_____

_____

_____

_____

3. Students should be looking for dates, names and incidents related to the topic you have identified. Be sure to alert them to resources or resource people who will be available to give them special help.

4. In the days after the visit(s), help the students organize the information chronologically and eliminate the duplicates.

5. Mount the ordered information forms on the roll of paper; this becomes your time line. If there are time periods or events which need further research, help the students find alternative information sources.

6. Display the time line prominently so that you can make frequent use of it as you continue your study.

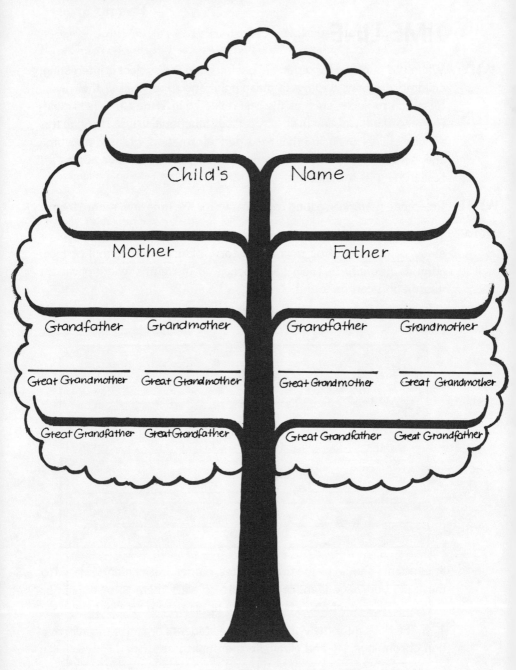

Family Tree

WHY: Reading information recorded by others and developing their own records will help children appreciate the importance these documents can serve in preserving information over time.

HOW: 1. As a family project, complete the accompanying "Family Tree"

2. Discuss the family history with your children and help them to be more aware of their "roots".

3. You might want to make reference to *Roots*, by Alex Haley, or point out how the *Little House* series serves to leave records about a family.

WHAT ELSE: Children might want to include the completed tree in a family history book with chapters for each generation and a page for each member that contains information, such as:

Name:

was born _____ died _____

place _____ place _____

education: _____

Important facts or things he or she should be remembered for:

_____

_____

_____

_____

_____

_____

HEADSTONES

WHY: Headstones preserve vital statistics of past generations. Sometimes epitaphs provide additional information about individuals' feelings or accomplishments. These are good examples of the way writing can communicate to people in the future.

WITH: Field trip to a historic battlefield, old cemetery, clipboards, paper and pencils.

HOW: 1. Along with your in-school activities related to a local history unit, arrange a field trip to a historic cemetery in your area or to an old battleground site that has a cemetery. Walk through the cemetery and read the headstones.

2. Children should record information from the headstones. You will probably want to structure this part of the activity (e.g., recording names, birthdates and deaths, etc.), but children may find additional information they want to note.

3. When you return to school, use the children's records as the basis for a discussion of the information the class acquired. These discussions may encompass a wide variety of topics (e.g., common names in a particular era; average life span of a former era compared to the present day; typical language patterns of a particular period of time).

Regarding Your Past

WHY: The value of written records in preserving the past is often rather abstract to children. Participating in an activity which involves family records provides a personally relevant example of this function of written language. Most of us have collections of family photographs or snapshots that we somehow never get to organize. Assembling, labeling and entering these in an album or scrapbook is an enjoyable family project which illustrates the value of print in preserving information over time.

HOW: 1. With your child, organize family photographs or snapshots in sequential order. For very old photos, you may need to ask grandparents or other relatives for help in identifying people, places and dates. Some newer photos give the month and year the film was developed; this information will be helpful.

2. Label the photos with important names, dates and places.

3. Mount photos using corners or use an album that doesn't require gluing photos to the page.

4. Let you child provide a caption under the photos after they are mounted.

5. Be sure to review the album. Share it with other relatives and friends.

SWAP SHOP

WHY: A practical example of writing intended to communicate with an absent audience is the writing used in advertising. Examining advertisements for popular items or services will help children recognize important features of this type of writing. An activity such as **Swap Shop** will provide a chance to do some composing that is likely to result in successfully "selling" a product.

WITH: Books, thumb-shaped paper, bulletin board, tokens.

HOW: 1. Have the students identify and bring in books they want to swap. For each book a student brings in, she or he receives a token to use in "buying" other books.

2. In order to help "sell" the books, students can advertise by writing a thumbnail sketch which includes a summary of the plot or describes the book's unusual or particularly interesting features. For each thumbnail sketch, the author receives one additional token.

3. Appoint a committee to price the books, using the thumbnail sketches as a guide. The author of the thumbnail sketch then receives as many tokens as the price assigned to the book. Books with no accompanying thumbnail sketch can be priced at one token.

SWAP SHOP
Tuesday, October 9

How to Swap	Books to Swap	Number of Tokens
1. Bring in book you want to swap.	1. Charlotte's Web	10
	2. Amelia Bedelia	5
2. Get a token for each book you bring.	3. The Great Gilly Hopkins	5
	4.	
	5.	
3 Get an extra token for writing a "thumbnail sketch".	6.	
	7.	
	8.	

4. Be sure to provide time for book browsing before the "sale".

5. On the designated day, children can sign up for the books they want to "buy".

WHAT ELSE:

1. It might be fun to have children use a number code rather than their names on the thumbnail sketches. You can keep the master list until the pricing day. This will also discourage personalities or friendships from influencing the pricing.

2. If more than one person wants to buy a particular book, it could be sold to the highest bidder—auction style.

3. Similarly, books that did not sell might be offered at a reduced price of two for one token.

4. Another activity using this type of writing might focus on advertising to "Hire a Volunteer" for help needed in the classroom. Students can write ads describing projects or activities which a parent or volunteer could supervise or help organize. A form or standard format including the job title, hours per week, and number of weeks or months might be developed. The job description should emphasize the positive features of the position, such as opportunity to work in a lively, exciting environment and hours which coordinate with the child's schedule.

Mystery Swap

WHY: Children need help and practice to learn how to be explicit with language. Activities like **Mystery Swap** described below provide motivating experiences in writing explicit information.

HOW: 1. Arrange with some friends or neighbors to join you in a "mystery swap" of some items in your homes which are still in good condition but are not currently in use.

2. With your child, make a list of words which describe each item you hope to swap. Use these word lists as the basis for a more complete description, a paragraph or so in length, which tells all about the mystery items *without naming them*. The other participants will need to prepare similar descriptions and choose the ones they want to swap for.

3. On the designated day, have everyone read the descriptions and choose the ones they want to swap for.

4. Before the final exchange, have participants guess what they think they will be getting. Have someone serve as secretary and write down these guesses to the items as each is identified.

About the Authors

Irene H. Blum, Ph.D., is co-author of many articles which have appeared in various reading journals that are concerned with the need of reading to be applicable to everyday situations. She is currently Project Director of a Basic Skills Parent Project and Research Associate, the Catholic University of America, School of Education. Dr. Blum studied at the University of Pennsylvania and University of Maryland, where she received her Doctor of Philosophy degree.

Nancy E. Taylor, Ph.D., has been published in numerous professional publications, among which are The Reading Teacher, Language Arts and Journal of Reading Behavior. She is a graduate of Hood College and received both her M.Ed and Ph.D. from University of Maryland. She is Associate Professor at the Catholic University of America, School of Education.

Priscilla Pilson Waynant is Adjunct Instructor, Loyola College, Baltimore, Maryland, and the George Mason University, Virginia. She received both her B.S. and M.Ed. degrees from the University of Maryland. She is co-author of "Reading logs reflect students real world reading need", published in The Reading Teacher and has written for Charles E. Merrill Publishing Company.

Bibliography

Brown, Ann. *Knowing When, Where and How to Remember: A Problem of Metacognition.* (Tech. Rep. No. 47) University of Illinois at Urbana-Champaign, The Center for the Study of Reading, June, 1977.

Carle, Eric. *Secret Birthday Message.* Thomas Y. Crowell Co., New York, 1972.

Carle, Eric. *Very Hungry Caterpillar.* Collins Publisher, Inc., New York, 1969.

Contemporary Motivators, Pendulum Press, Double Play Kits; Triple Play Kits. Bowmar/Noble, Los Angeles, California.

Downing, J. *Reading and reasoning.* Springer-Verlag Inc., New York, 1979.

Downing, J. & Thackray, D. *Reading Readiness.* Hodder and Stoughton, London, 1978.

Emberly, Barbara. *Drummer Hoff.* Prentice-Hall, Inc., Englewood Cliffs, N.J., 1969.

Galdone, Paul. *The Three Bears.* Scholastic Book Services, New York, 1973.

Goodman, K.S. & Goodman, Y.M. Learning to read is natural. L.B. Resnick and P.A. Weaver (Eds.), *Theory and practice of early reading* (Vol. 1). Laurence Erlbaum Associates, Hillsdale, N.J., 1979.

Hiebert, Elfrieda. *The development of reading-related knowledge over the pre-school years.* Paper presented at the meeting of the American Educational Research Association, Boston, April, 1980.

Hillert, Margaret. *The Three Bears.* Follett Publishing Co., Chicago.

Hoban, Tana. *Count and See.* MacMillan Publishing Co., New York, 1972.

Jacobs, Joseph, Trans. by Walser, David. *Jack and the Beanstalk.* Thomas Y. Crowell Co., New York, 1978.

Lewis, Gail & Shaw, Jean. *Recipes for Learning.* Goodyear Publishing Co., Santa Monica, CA, 1979.

Martin, Bill & Brogan, Peggy. *Instant Readers*. Holt, Rinehart and Winston, Inc., New York, 1970.

Madsen, S. & Gould, B. *The Teacher's Book of Lists*. Goodyear Publishing Co., Santa Monica, CA, 1979.

Munston, D. *The Canning and Freezing Book*. The Culinary Arts Institute, Chicago, 1975.

Ollila, Lloyd O. Handbook for administrators and teachers. *Reading in the Kindergarten*. International Reading Association, Newark, Delaware, 1980.

Potter, Beatrix. *Peter Rabbit*. Nursery Treasury Books, 1962.

READ ALONG - READ ALONE 1971. Scott Foresman, Glenview, Il 60024

Ruben, Patricia. *Apples to Zippers*. Doubleday and Company, Inc., Garden City, N.Y., 1976.

Scott Foresman Talking Story Book Box: "Ask Mr. Bear", "Brownie", "Goggles", "The Wild Duck and the Goose", "M is for Moving", "Just Me", "Joey's Cat".

Sendak, Maurice. *Chicken Soup with Rice*. Harper and Row Publishers, Inc., New York, 1970.

Smith, Frank. "Making sense of reading—and reading instruction". Harvard Educational Review, *47*, August, 1977, 386-395.

Smith, Frank. *Reading Without Nonsense*. Teachers College Press, New York, 1979.

Smith, Frank. "The use of language", *Language Arts, 1977 (b), 54, 6, 638-644.*

Steig, William. *The Amazing Bone*. Puffin Books, New York, 1977.

Steig, William. *Sylvester and the Magic Pebble*. Windmill Books and E.P. Dutton, New York, 1969.

Taylor, N.E., and Vawter, J.M. "Helping children discover the functions of written language". *Language Arts, 1978, 55, 941-945.*

Wells, Rosemary. *Noisy Nora*. Scholastic Book Services, New York, 1973.